Prologue

Hurricane Helene swept through Asheville, altering the landscape of our lives in unimaginable ways. As a resident directly affected by the storm, I witnessed the chaos and destruction firsthand. Homes were damaged, and community bonds were tested. Yet amid the turmoil, a spirit of resilience emerged. This book captures the personal stories of recovery, the challenges we faced, and the unwavering support from our neighbors. It is a testament to our journey—a reminder that even in the face of adversity, we can rise stronger together.

Hurricane Helene:

Memoirs from Asheville, NC

Written by

Maya Rivers

Introduction

Hurricane Helene, which made its presence felt in September 2024, is a chapter of history that profoundly impacted the city of Asheville, North Carolina. While the storm originated as a formidable Category 3 hurricane in the Atlantic, its eventual trajectory led to a much different outcome for Asheville and its surrounding areas. The storm weakened significantly before making landfall, but it nonetheless brought torrential rains, gusty winds, and a sense of impending doom that resonated deeply within the community.

In the days leading up to Hurricane Helene, a palpable tension enveloped Asheville. Local news stations provided constant updates, weather alerts flooded our phones, and conversations turned from mundane topics to discussions about preparedness and safety. Residents scoured grocery stores for essentials, filling their carts with water, batteries, canned goods, and other supplies, often sharing anxious glances and exchanging stories about previous storms. The atmosphere was thick with apprehension and a sense of urgency, yet there was also an undercurrent of community spirit as neighbors came together to compare notes and offer help to those who were less prepared.

As a resident who lived through those pivotal days, my personal connection to Hurricane Helene is woven into the fabric of my own life story. I vividly recall the murmur of conversations in my neighborhood as families prepared for the worst. My parents, seasoned in their own ways, relied on their instincts and past experiences with storms to guide our preparations. I can still see my father in the garage, methodically stacking flashlights and batteries, while my mother monitored the latest forecasts. Their calm amidst the chaos provided a sense of reassurance, but the reality of the situation was never far from my mind. "We'll be okay," they said, but the uncertainty loomed like a shadow over our household.

When Helene finally arrived, it did not unleash the full force of its initial potential, but the storm brought its own set of challenges. The heavy rains caused local rivers to swell, leading to flash flooding that would sweep through familiar neighborhoods, transforming roads into rivers and homes into shelters of despair. I vividly recall standing at my window, watching as the winds howled and rain lashed against the glass, nature's fury manifesting just beyond our safety. In that moment, the world outside became a tempestuous reminder of how small and fragile we are in the face of such overwhelming power. I remember glancing out at the trees bending violently against the wind, their branches snapping like twigs, and feeling a surge of adrenaline mixed with fear.

In the immediate aftermath of the storm, the chaos unfolded like a scene from a movie. As the winds subsided and the rain turned to a drizzle, I ventured outside, my heart racing with anticipation. The sight was surreal: streets transformed into rivers, debris scattered like confetti, and the familiar landscape of Asheville altered beyond recognition. I remember the faces of my neighbors, a mixture of shock and determination etched into their features. Conversations echoed around me, sharing news of flooded basements and damaged roofs, each story amplifying the urgency of our new reality.

The community response was nothing short of inspiring. Neighbors reached out to help one another, clearing debris, checking on the elderly, and offering shelter to those whose homes were damaged. There was a profound sense of unity as people put aside their differences and came together to rebuild not only their physical surroundings but also their collective spirit. I witnessed acts of kindness that resonated deeply, reinforcing the idea that even in the wake of devastation, hope can emerge. I remember watching the Thompson family, who lived two houses down, rally their friends to help clear the road of fallen trees. Their children, who had once played together in the summer sun, now worked side by side, equipped with saws and gloves, as laughter cut through the tension of the moment.

This memoir aims to chronicle the multifaceted experiences surrounding Hurricane Helene—capturing the anxiety before the storm, the intensity during the hurricane, and the resilience of our community in its aftermath. It is a tribute to the people of Asheville, whose strength and solidarity were tested and ultimately reaffirmed during this tumultuous time. Through shared stories, reflections, and lessons learned, I hope to convey the indelible impact of Hurricane Helene on our lives and the enduring spirit of a community that emerged stronger on the other side.

Chapter 1: The Calm Before the Storm

Asheville, North Carolina, is renowned for its stunning natural beauty, framed by the majestic Blue Ridge Mountains. The temperate climate, marked by warm summers and crisp autumns, makes it a beloved destination for residents and tourists alike. However, despite its idyllic surroundings, Asheville is not immune to the unpredictable forces of nature. Severe weather events, while infrequent, can disrupt the rhythm of daily life and instill a palpable sense of anxiety within the community. The approach of a hurricane, in particular, is a catalyst for heightened awareness and preparation among the town's residents.

In the days leading up to Hurricane Helene, Asheville began to pulse with a collective sense of urgency. Local meteorologists monitored the storm's trajectory as it churned in the Atlantic, and forecasts became increasingly dire. Conversations shifted from light-hearted exchanges about weekend plans to serious discussions about safety and preparation. Many residents, having lived through previous storms, understood the potential for disruption and damage that a hurricane could bring. Familiar faces in the community began to engage in discussions that underscored a shared concern for the well-being of their families and neighbors.

At the local grocery store, the atmosphere buzzed with activity. Shelves that typically held canned goods and bottled water were quickly emptied as families stocked up on essentials. In an aisle lined with non-perishable items, a mother with two children in tow hurriedly tossed boxes of macaroni and cheese into her cart. "I just want to be prepared," she said, her voice tinged with urgency. Other shoppers nodded in agreement, echoing her sentiments as they navigated the frantic scene.

An elderly man in a baseball cap observed the chaos with a furrowed brow. He had lived in Asheville for decades and remembered the devastation of past storms. "This feels different," he muttered to a nearby shopper. "We need to take this seriously." His words resonated with those around him, reinforcing the communal understanding that preparation was essential.

As the countdown to Hurricane Helene continued, the energy in Asheville shifted from anxiety to action. Neighbors organized to help one another, gathering supplies and sharing resources. In the heart of the city, a group of college students joined forces to create care packages for vulnerable community members. They packed non-perishable food items, flashlights, and hygiene supplies, ensuring that everyone would be taken care of in the face of uncertainty. "It's important that we all look out for each other," one student remarked as they worked together.

In the local hardware store, similar scenes unfolded. Residents lined up to purchase plywood, nails, and tools for securing outdoor furniture. The lines stretched long as families prepared their homes for the storm. Conversations buzzed with camaraderie, as strangers exchanged stories and advice. "Have you ever boarded up windows before?" one man asked another. "Let me show you how," came the friendly reply, emphasizing the sense of community that emerged in the face of adversity.

Amidst the flurry of activity, social media platforms erupted with posts urging residents to prepare. Local authorities shared tips on how to stay safe and check on neighbors, especially those who were elderly or living alone. The hashtag #AshevilleStrong began circulating, embodying the community's spirit as they rallied together in anticipation of the storm. Residents posted updates, sharing their own preparations while encouraging others to do the same. "Let's make sure everyone is ready," one post read, highlighting the interconnectedness of the community.

As the storm drew closer, the atmosphere in Asheville was a mixture of hope and apprehension. Families gathered in their living rooms, watching the news updates and discussing their plans. "What will we do if the power goes out?" one child asked, looking up at his parents with wide eyes. They assured him that they would be okay, promising to light candles and tell stories if necessary. The emotional landscape was painted with a sense of resilience, as families came together to confront the unknown.

At the same time, local schools began to send out notifications about closures and emergency preparedness plans. Teachers discussed safety protocols with their students, transforming classroom discussions into lessons about resilience and community support. "We need to be ready for anything," one teacher emphasized, fostering a sense of responsibility among her students. This proactive approach extended beyond the schools; community centers opened their doors to those who needed shelter or assistance, reinforcing the message that no one would be left behind.

The sense of anticipation grew stronger as Hurricane Helene approached, intertwining the threads of fear, determination, and community. Residents began to feel a connection to one another, a bond forged through shared experiences and a common goal: to weather the storm safely and together. In these moments, as the town readied itself for the onslaught of nature, the spirit of Asheville shone brightly.

As night fell, the skies darkened ominously, casting a shadow over the town. Residents tucked themselves into bed, their thoughts racing with concern and hope. Many knew the challenges they faced in the coming days, but the knowledge that they were part of a supportive community provided solace. In the face of adversity, the people of Asheville were more than mere individuals; they were a collective force, ready to embrace the trials ahead with unwavering determination.

With each tick of the clock, the reality of Hurricane Helene loomed closer. Asheville, often characterized by its serene beauty, now stood at the precipice of a significant natural event. The community prepared not just for the storm itself, but for the subsequent challenges and triumphs that would unfold in its wake. The calm before the storm, while filled with tension, also echoed with a powerful sense of unity—a reminder that together, they could face whatever the hurricane would bring.

Chapter 2: The Arrival of Hurricane Helene

As the hours ticked down to the arrival of Hurricane Helene, Asheville buzzed with an electricity that felt almost palpable. The once-familiar sounds of the city—the laughter of children playing outside, the hum of cars on the road, the friendly chatter in cafes—were slowly replaced by an undercurrent of anxiety. Local meteorologists provided updates with an urgency that amplified the tension, emphasizing the storm's unpredictable nature. Each bulletin felt like a countdown, and the community was gripped by a mixture of fear and determination.

In the days leading up to the hurricane, weather reports shifted rapidly. Initially, it was forecasted that Helene would weaken as it approached the Blue Ridge Mountains, but as the storm's path became clearer, predictions began to change. Suddenly, residents were warned of heavy rainfall, possible flash flooding, and winds that could reach dangerous levels. The realization set in that this was not just another storm; it was a force of nature that could bring destruction to their beloved town.

Local news stations filled the airwaves with updates, offering not only forecasts but also survival tips. The newscasters became familiar faces, their voices a constant reminder of the impending storm. "Prepare for the worst, hope for the best," one anchor advised, and those words echoed through homes as families gathered to discuss their plans. The palpable tension transformed coffee shops, grocery stores, and public spaces into hubs of concern. Conversations shifted from light banter to urgent discussions about supplies and preparations, revealing the community's shared anxiety.

One notable story emerged from the Anderson family, long-time residents of Asheville. They had weathered their share of storms over the years, and when they heard the news about Helene, they were reminded of Hurricane Fran, which had left a lasting impression on their home and family. "We're not going to be caught off guard this time," said John Anderson, a father of three. The family decided to take proactive measures, transforming their garage into a staging area for emergency supplies. As they worked together, their children, Emily and Sam, collected flashlights, batteries, and non-perishable food items. The sense of urgency and responsibility resonated with them, and even the youngest, four-year-old Lily, felt a sense of pride as she helped fill bags with snacks.

Meanwhile, across town, the Martinez family faced a different challenge. New to the area, they had never experienced a hurricane before. Ana Martinez, a mother of two, felt the anxiety swell within her as she watched her neighbors hustle about. "What do we need to do?" she wondered aloud as she scrolled through social media, absorbing the advice shared by more seasoned locals. Her husband, Miguel, had lived through hurricanes in his native Puerto Rico, and although storms were not foreign to him, the mountainous terrain of Asheville felt unnerving. "We'll be okay," he assured her, but even he felt the weight of uncertainty. Together, they ventured to the local grocery store, where the shelves were beginning to empty. Ana pushed the cart, her heart racing as they stocked up on water, canned goods, and dry snacks. In the back of her mind, she thought of her neighbors and how they might fare during the storm.

As the storm drew closer, the sense of urgency became a community-wide phenomenon. The streets were filled with the sound of hammers and nails as neighbors banded together to board up windows and secure outdoor furniture. The power of community spirit was evident; even those who had never interacted before found common ground in their shared determination to protect their homes. In the heart of downtown Asheville, the owners of a popular local café, "The Blue Ridge Brew," worked tirelessly to secure their outdoor patio. Maria, the owner, had gathered her staff for an emergency meeting. "We need to make sure everything is locked down," she said, her voice steady despite the fear bubbling beneath the surface. The team rallied together, quickly boarding up windows and moving furniture inside.

In the midst of the preparations, acts of kindness flourished. The Thompson family, whose father was deployed overseas, found themselves in a tight spot. They had planned to spend the storm at home but realized they might need extra hands. As news spread, neighbors rallied to offer their help. "We can help you board up," said one neighbor, a retired firefighter, as he grabbed a toolbox. His daughter, a college student home for the break, joined in as they tackled the task together, transforming an intimidating situation into a community bonding experience.

Throughout Asheville, the atmosphere was thick with both anxiety and resolve. People reached out to one another, sharing resources, tips, and emotional support. On a local Facebook group, posts filled with offers for food and shelter flooded the feed. "If anyone needs a place to stay, our doors are open," one neighbor wrote, while another shared a list of emergency supplies. The community's resilience shone through in those moments, a testament to the strength found in unity.

As the wind began to howl and the first heavy raindrops fell, the collective spirit of Asheville became a beacon of hope. The city stood together, fortified by the knowledge that they would face Hurricane Helene as a united front. This chapter captures the essence of the storm's arrival, illustrating not only the frantic preparations made by families and businesses but also the emotional landscape of a community confronting a formidable natural disaster.

The fear, determination, and camaraderie among residents painted a portrait of resilience that would define their experience in the days to come. The strength they found in each other became the very foundation of their hope as they braced for the tempest ahead.

As darkness enveloped the city, anticipation reached a fever pitch. The sky, once filled with the fading light of the day, now swirled with ominous clouds, a harbinger of the chaos that would soon unfold. Residents watched from their windows, some gripping their children tightly, others whispering reassurances to loved ones. The community was no longer simply preparing for a storm; they were bracing for a significant life event that would test their resolve and redefine their connections to one another.

In the early hours of the morning, as the winds began to pick up, families huddled together, glued to their radios and screens for updates. The sound of the weather radio crackling to life was both comforting and alarming. "This is your local station reporting live. The eye of Hurricane Helene is projected to make landfall in the next few hours," the announcer's voice boomed, a stark reminder that they were at the mercy of nature's fury.

The Anderson family settled into their living room, illuminated by the soft glow of battery-powered lanterns. "This is just like a sleepover, right?" joked Sam, trying to lighten the mood. Emily rolled her eyes, but she couldn't help but smile. "Yeah, except there's a hurricane outside!"

Meanwhile, the Martinez family huddled in their kitchen, surrounded by their provisions. Miguel reminisced about the tropical storms of his childhood, but he quickly dismissed the thought. "This is different," he noted, glancing at Ana, whose anxiety was palpable. "We'll get through this together."

As the wind howled outside, it began to batter against windows, a chilling reminder of what lay ahead. In the ensuing hours, the atmosphere shifted dramatically. What began as nervous excitement morphed into sheer determination as residents braced for impact. Their resolve crystallized in moments of shared laughter, shared fear, and shared hope.

As Hurricane Helene approached Asheville, it brought with it not just destruction but also an opportunity for growth, connection, and resilience. Little did they know, the events that would unfold over the coming days would redefine their community in ways they could not yet imagine. The storm was no longer just a weather event; it was a catalyst for transformation, a testament to the strength of the human spirit, and a reminder of the power of unity in the face of adversity.

Chapter 3: The Eye of the Storm

As Hurricane Helene drew closer, the atmosphere in Asheville buzzed with an ominous energy, charged with anticipation and fear. The sound of wind and rain began to resonate in the hearts of its residents, creating a rhythm that mirrored their anxious pulses. Families huddled in their living rooms, eyes glued to television screens, watching local meteorologists trace the storm's relentless path. Each update amplified the urgency of the moment, layering the air with an unshakeable sense of impending chaos.

With the storm intensifying, local news reports shifted from measured warnings to urgent appeals for safety. The beloved meteorologist, known for his warm demeanor and calm reassurances, now appeared grave as he delivered the latest updates. "This is not just another storm; we are looking at a serious weather event," he stated, his voice steady yet tinged with concern as he detailed the rapidly escalating winds and potential for significant flooding. Residents felt the weight of his words settle over them like a heavy blanket, anxiety mingling with determination as they prepared for the worst.

In the Anderson home, a sense of organization mixed with anxiety filled the air. They had transformed their living room into a makeshift shelter, gathering supplies—flashlights, batteries, canned goods, and even a deck of cards to distract the children from the looming storm. "We've been through storms before," John reassured his wife, Sarah, though the knot of worry tightened in his stomach. "We'll be fine." He forced a smile for their children, trying to maintain a facade of strength. Emily and Sam exchanged glances, sensing the undercurrents of fear that flowed through their parents.

Meanwhile, Ana and Miguel Martinez sought refuge at a local community center converted into an emergency shelter. The reality that they had never faced a hurricane hung over them like a dark cloud. "We are in the unknown," Ana whispered, glancing around at the families surrounding them. Anxiety was palpable, echoed in the faces of others who, like them, were navigating this treacherous territory for the first time. Miguel, drawing on distant memories of storms from his childhood in Puerto Rico, attempted to comfort Ana, yet he too felt the gravity of the moment. "We'll get through this together," he said, forcing a reassuring smile even as doubt flickered in his eyes.

As the wind began to howl and the first heavy rains cascaded down, many residents ventured to their porches or windows, drawn by the storm's growing fury. What was once a serene mountain town morphed into a scene of chaos. Branches cracked, and trees swayed violently, their roots straining against the deluge. For those watching, the sight was both terrifying and mesmerizing. The air buzzed with the sound of nature's wrath, creating a visceral reminder of their vulnerability.

In the moments before the storm reached its peak, an eerie calm settled over the town. Families gathered closely, listening to the radio or watching the news as the wind grew louder, drowning out their voices. The anticipation of what lay ahead weighed heavily in the air, thick with uncertainty. The Anderson children, clutching each other on the couch, sensed their parents' unease, which only heightened their own anxiety.

When the storm finally made landfall, it did so with a ferocity that shattered any remaining sense of security. The wind screamed through the streets of Asheville, rattling windows and sending debris hurtling through the air. The quiet neighborhoods transformed into battlegrounds against the elements. Trees toppled, crashing against homes and cars, while power lines snapped with loud cracks that echoed like thunderclaps.

Amidst the chaos, emergency services mobilized. The Asheville Fire Department, equipped for such crises, deployed units throughout the city, ready to respond to emergencies. Firefighters and police officers braved the tempest, aware that lives depended on their ability to reach those in distress. "Just keep the lines open!" shouted Captain Harris, rallying his team. "We need to be ready for anything." The urgency in his voice resonated with his crew, who had trained for scenarios like this, yet the reality of the storm pushed them to their limits. Their radios crackled with distress calls from residents, each plea amplifying the weight of responsibility they carried.

As hurricane-force winds howled, power outages swept through Asheville, plunging entire neighborhoods into darkness. The comforting hum of modern life vanished, replaced by the howling winds and the relentless rain battering against rooftops. Families resorted to flashlights and candles, their flickering lights casting ghostly shadows on the walls. The absence of electricity transformed the experience into something surreal, as if time itself had stopped.

Within the emergency shelter, the atmosphere was a mix of anxiety and resilience. Families congregated in large rooms, sharing stories to distract themselves from the storm's fury outside. Laughter and chatter filled the space, providing a semblance of comfort amid the chaos. A local volunteer circulated with blankets and snacks, distributing them to families huddled together. "You're not alone," she said, her smile warm and genuine. "We're all in this together."

Despite the camaraderie within the shelter, concerns about safety loomed large. As wind gusts intensified, fears about flooding grew. Water began to seep into the building, prompting a swift response from volunteers. "We need to move everyone to the second floor!" shouted a Red Cross worker. Panic rippled through the crowd, but the calmness of the staff helped restore order. Families quickly gathered their belongings, hearts racing as they climbed to safety.

Outside, the storm raged on. Streets transformed into rivers, flooding cars and isolating neighborhoods. First responders faced formidable challenges navigating the treacherous conditions, with some roads rendered impassable. The bravery of emergency teams shone through in these moments, as they maneuvered through the rising waters to rescue those stranded in their homes. "Keep your heads up; we're coming for you!" a firefighter shouted through the rain, using a megaphone to guide trapped residents. His voice cut through the din of the storm, offering hope to those who felt abandoned. Meanwhile, other emergency responders used boats to reach families who had taken refuge on rooftops.

As hours turned into what felt like days, the community held its collective breath, hoping the worst was behind them. News reports began to highlight the scale of the damage across the region, with images of uprooted trees and flooded streets dominating local broadcasts. The shared anxiety among residents grew as they awaited updates on the storm's trajectory and the extent of the destruction.

Despite the turmoil, acts of kindness flourished. Neighbors who had never spoken before found common ground, helping one another clean up debris and check on the well-being of those around them. In a neighborhood where people often kept to themselves, bonds formed in the wake of the storm. "We'll get through this together," said one resident as he helped an elderly neighbor clear fallen branches. His words echoed the sentiment shared by many, a powerful reminder of the strength that comes from unity.

As the storm's intensity began to wane, the aftermath of Hurricane Helene revealed a new reality. Families emerged from their homes to a landscape transformed by nature's fury. Roads were littered with debris, and the sounds of chainsaws echoed as residents began the arduous task of recovery. Neighbors banded together, using their collective strength to clear the path forward, literally and metaphorically.

In the days to come, Asheville would face the challenges of recovery and rebuilding. Yet, in that moment, amid the winds and rain, they lived through a shared experience that would bond them forever. The stories of courage, compassion, and resilience would unfold in the aftermath, creating a narrative that showcased the spirit of a community determined to rise above the challenges posed by nature's wrath.

Chapter 4: The Aftermath

As dawn broke after the fury of Hurricane Helene, Asheville emerged into a changed world. The air was thick with humidity, mingling with the scent of rain-soaked earth and broken branches. Residents tentatively stepped outside, the early morning light revealing a landscape transformed by the storm's relentless power. Initial reactions were a medley of disbelief, relief, and an instinctual drive to assess the damage. Some ventured into their yards, faces pale and drawn, struggling to comprehend the scene before them.

For the Anderson family, the morning light illuminated a yard strewn with debris—branches, leaves, and parts of their beloved treehouse lay scattered like forgotten toys. John and Sarah exchanged worried glances as their children, Emily and Sam, began to cry. "It's all gone," Emily lamented, pointing at what remained of their childhood play space. Her younger sister, Lily, clutched her favorite stuffed animal tightly, as if it could somehow shield her from the disappointment. Sarah knelt beside her children, reassuring them, "It's okay, we'll rebuild. We can fix this together." Her words, filled with love and determination, were meant to anchor her children in the storm's aftermath.

Nearby, the Martinez family grappled with a mixture of shock and anxiety. Ana, still reeling from the storm, surveyed the scene. Downed power lines snaked across the street, and debris was piled high on sidewalks. "This isn't what I expected," she murmured, heart racing as she scrolled through social media, desperately seeking news and guidance. Miguel, having faced hurricanes in Puerto Rico, felt a sense of unease wash over him. "We've made it through storms before, but this feels different," he admitted, furrowing his brows as he tried to find the right words to comfort his wife.

The neighborhoods surrounding Asheville, including smaller towns like Weaverville and Black Mountain, also grappled with the aftermath. Reports began to trickle in about the extent of flooding in these areas, where rivers had overflowed their banks, inundating homes and businesses. In Weaverville, the local library, a beloved community hub, was partially submerged, its shelves lined with soggy books. Residents flocked to the town square, sharing their own stories of loss and resilience. "We never expected this kind of damage," one elderly woman remarked, voice trembling as she pointed to the water line on her porch.

As the sun climbed higher, community members began to emerge, many equipped with tools and determination. First responders and local volunteers quickly mobilized, ready to assess the damage and lend a helping hand. Captain Harris and his team were already out on the streets, driving through neighborhoods in their emergency vehicles. "We need to check for any trapped individuals or those in need of medical assistance," he said, voice resolute. The first priority was ensuring the safety of residents, particularly the elderly and vulnerable.

Local news stations filled the airwaves with live updates, broadcasting images of destruction and the community's efforts to restore order. Drones soared overhead, capturing aerial footage of the devastation. Roads were clogged with fallen trees, and homes that once stood proud now showed signs of extensive damage. "Asheville is facing an uphill battle," one reporter stated, echoing the sentiments of many residents. The camera panned to the Biltmore Estate, where large trees had toppled, their roots exposed—a visual testament to the storm's fury.

The flooding affected the region in ways that were not immediately visible. The Swannanoa River swelled beyond its banks, leading to significant flooding in areas near the river. Houses that had been untouched during previous storms were now inundated, water creeping into basements and lower levels. The community banded together to rescue those trapped, launching small boats to reach stranded families. "This is the worst I've seen in years," said one volunteer as he maneuvered through the debris-laden water, determination etched on his face.

As the dust began to settle, the need for community support became clear. Social media transformed into a lifeline, with residents sharing their needs and offers of assistance. "I have extra water and canned goods," one post read. "If anyone needs supplies, let me know." In another thread, a neighbor offered shelter to those who had lost power. "Our doors are open, and we have room," they posted—a beacon of hope amidst the chaos.

In the heart of downtown, local businesses became centers of recovery. Maria, owner of "The Blue Ridge Brew," gathered her staff early that morning. "We need to assess the damage and help the community," she said, tone a mix of urgency and optimism. "Let's prepare to serve meals to those in need. People are going to need nourishment, both physically and emotionally." The café's staff quickly organized, turning their focus from business to community support. They set up tables outside, offering coffee, pastries, and warm meals to anyone who stopped by, creating a welcoming atmosphere in a time of despair.

As the sun rose higher, the sounds of chainsaws and hammers filled the air. Neighbors united in a remarkable display of solidarity, banding together to clear streets and assist those whose homes were damaged. The Thompson family, whose father was deployed overseas, found themselves in need of help. "We were planning to hunker down and ride it out, but this is too much for us to handle alone," said Amanda, the mother. Word quickly spread, and soon, neighbors rallied to their side, transforming an overwhelming task into a shared effort.

"Let's get your trees cleared first," suggested one neighbor, a retired firefighter with experience in storm recovery. His teenage daughter joined him, quickly becoming a symbol of resilience in the community. As they worked, other families arrived, bringing tools and enthusiasm. The atmosphere was electric with a sense of purpose, as residents shared stories and laughter amidst the debris. "We'll make this better together," one woman said, her voice carrying hope that lifted spirits.

Yet amidst the recovery, the challenges loomed large. Power outages persisted across Asheville, leaving many residents without electricity for days. The grocery stores that had been stripped bare before the storm faced logistical nightmares, struggling to restock as delivery routes remained disrupted. Lines formed outside stores, with residents anxiously awaiting their turn to grab essentials—a stark reminder of the storm's impact.

Residents in nearby towns faced similar struggles, as many were left without running water or electricity. In Black Mountain, a popular festival set to take place was postponed due to the storm's devastation. Local leaders met to discuss their communities' needs and how best to support one another. "We're all in this together," said the mayor of Black Mountain, urging residents to help one another through these tough times.

As the sun set, the physical toll of the storm became apparent, but so did the emotional strain. The community grappled not only with property damage but also with the psychological aftermath of the hurricane. Mental health professionals mobilized, offering support and counseling services to those affected. "This is a critical time for our community," said a local therapist, echoing many thoughts. "People need to know it's okay to ask for help."

Gradually, grassroots activism emerged, with residents organizing cleanup events and recovery efforts. The Anderson family, inspired by their neighbors' kindness, spearheaded a community cleanup initiative. They posted flyers around the neighborhood, inviting residents to come together. "We can't do this alone," John stated, his voice steady with resolve. "But if we work together, we can make a difference."

As the weeks turned into months, the road to recovery proved long and arduous. Each day presented new challenges, but the community stood firm. The aftermath of Hurricane Helene would not only be defined by the damage inflicted but also by the stories of resilience, compassion, and hope that emerged in the face of adversity. The connections forged through shared experiences would serve as a testament to the strength of Asheville, transforming the aftermath into an opportunity for renewal and growth.

In the end, it was the spirit of unity that would carry them forward as residents navigated the path to restoration, rebuilding not just their homes but also the bonds that would sustain them through the trials ahead. The collective memory of Hurricane Helene would linger, a powerful reminder of their capacity to come together in times of crisis, illustrating the enduring strength of community amidst nature's unpredictable forces.

Chapter 5: Personal Recovery Stories

As Asheville emerged from the chaos of Hurricane Helene, the resilience of its residents began to unfold in remarkable ways. The aftermath of the storm, marked by challenges and unexpected blessings, offered a window into the strength of community and the human spirit. Stories of recovery and support filled the air, weaving a rich tapestry of hope amid the wreckage.

Resilience

For the Anderson family, the storm had tested their mettle. John and Sarah Anderson, long-time Asheville residents, had weathered their share of storms, but Hurricane Helene was different. Their home, nestled at the foot of the mountains, bore the brunt of the storm's fury. A towering oak tree, once a cherished landmark in their yard, had crashed down, smashing the swing set and damaging their roof. Initially devastated, the family quickly resolved to take control of their recovery.

"We couldn't just sit around feeling sorry for ourselves," John declared, gathering his wife and three children in their living room. They formed a plan to tackle the cleanup together, emphasizing teamwork and a positive attitude. Each Saturday, they donned their work gloves and set out to restore their home. The children, Emily, Sam, and little Lily, took on various roles: Emily, a budding project manager at just ten years old, charted a course of action, while Sam took responsibility for picking up sticks and branches, turning it into a friendly competition. Lily, at four, decorated the debris piles with colorful drawings on paper plates, her innocent creativity bringing lightness to the task.

Despite the physical labor, the Andersons turned the cleanup process into a family bonding experience. "We played music, took breaks, and made it fun," Sarah recalled with a smile. "It was our way of coping with the loss." They would pause for impromptu dance parties in the yard, laughter replacing tears as they celebrated small victories like clearing a patch of grass or fixing a broken fence. Through their shared effort, the family learned valuable lessons about resilience, togetherness, and the importance of maintaining a positive outlook, even in dire circumstances.

Across town, the Martinez family navigated a different kind of recovery. Ana and Miguel had moved to Asheville just months before the hurricane, eager to start anew in a community that felt foreign yet inviting. As the storm approached, they found themselves caught between anxiety and the unfamiliarity of their new surroundings. After Helene passed, they faced their own set of challenges, with their home sustaining water damage from the heavy rainfall.

Determined to build connections in their new community, Ana took the initiative to organize a neighborhood block party to thank those who had supported them during the recovery. "We were overwhelmed by the generosity of our neighbors," Ana said, reflecting on the countless volunteers who had shown up to help clean and repair their home. "I wanted to bring everyone together to celebrate that support."

The block party became a catalyst for community bonding. Families shared food, stories, and laughter, turning an experience marked by uncertainty into one filled with hope. Miguel, who had lived through hurricanes in Puerto Rico, found solace in knowing they were not alone. "We learned that we are all connected," he explained. "The storm showed us the importance of community." The event transformed into a hub of shared experiences, where neighbors recounted their struggles and successes, strengthening the fabric of the neighborhood.

Community Bonding

The spirit of community support thrived in the wake of the storm. Across Asheville and the surrounding areas, neighbors stepped up to assist those who had lost more than just possessions. In Weaverville, a small town just north of Asheville, residents rallied together to provide aid for those whose homes were severely damaged. The local church, led by Pastor Jim, became a center for recovery efforts. "We turned our church basement into a distribution center," he said. "People came with food, clothing, and other essentials. It was a remarkable show of support."

Asheville's residents, fueled by a shared purpose, began to volunteer their time and resources. Many who had experienced previous storms felt compelled to give back. "I remember when I needed help after a flood a few years back," one local volunteer shared. "Now it's my turn to help others. That's how community works." This sentiment echoed through the streets as people formed teams to assist with cleanups, repairs, and resource distribution.

The Thompson family, who had been preparing for a quiet weekend, suddenly found themselves at the center of community efforts. With their father deployed overseas, Amanda Thompson and her children realized they needed assistance after their home suffered roof damage. "The outpouring of help was incredible," Amanda recalled. Neighbors arrived with tools and expertise, working together to patch the roof and ensure the family was safe. "It was heartwarming to see our neighbors step in," she said, a mixture of gratitude and disbelief in her voice. "Families brought us meals, helped clean up, and just checked in on us."

Acts of kindness flourished as residents supported one another. The local school organized a supply drive for families affected by the storm. Teachers and students came together to gather school supplies, clothing, and non-perishable food items. "It was heartwarming to see the children taking part in this," said Mrs. Jenkins, a beloved teacher. "They understood that we needed to support one another, especially the kids who lost so much."

The recovery efforts in Asheville extended beyond the city limits, impacting smaller surrounding towns. News reports emerged detailing the extensive flooding in towns like Marshall and Black Mountain, where homes were submerged, and roads washed out. "We've seen so much destruction," one resident from Black Mountain shared in a local news interview. "But we've also seen the community come together like never before."

In these small towns, residents faced their own struggles, but the same spirit of resilience shone brightly. Community centers opened their doors as shelters for those displaced by the floods. Volunteers from Asheville made the trek to help their neighbors, bringing food and supplies. "It's a reminder that we are all in this together," said a volunteer from Asheville who traveled to Black Mountain to lend assistance. "No one should have to face this alone."

Lessons Learned

As the immediate crisis subsided, residents began to reflect on the lessons learned from their experiences during and after Hurricane Helene. The storm served as a powerful reminder of the importance of preparedness. Many families began reassessing their emergency plans. The Andersons, for instance, recognized the need for a more organized approach. "We created a checklist of supplies and mapped out evacuation routes," Sarah noted. "It was a valuable exercise that brought us closer together as a family."

The Martinez family, having weathered the storm, became passionate advocates for community preparedness. They attended workshops on disaster readiness, eager to equip themselves with knowledge for future emergencies. "We didn't know what to expect, and now we want to make sure others are ready," Ana said. Their proactive approach extended beyond their family; they began sharing information with neighbors, emphasizing the importance of communication and planning.

Social media played a crucial role in keeping the community informed and connected. Local groups emerged, where residents shared resources, recovery updates, and support. "It became a lifeline," Ana said. "People were posting about what they needed, and others would respond almost immediately. It was heartening to see the generosity of our neighbors."

As recovery efforts continued, many residents began exploring long-term community projects aimed at building resilience against future disasters. Town meetings were held, focusing on improving infrastructure and emergency response systems. The community discussed creating gardens to promote sustainability, food security, and collaboration among residents. "We want to create something positive out of this experience," Amanda Thompson emphasized, her determination evident.

In this atmosphere of hope and renewal, the stories of personal recovery became intertwined with the collective narrative of Asheville and its surrounding towns. Each individual journey contributed to a larger narrative of resilience and community strength. The strength they found in one another became the foundation of their hope as they continued to heal.

Chapter 6: Long-Term Effects

As the dust began to settle from Hurricane Helene's aftermath, the long-term effects on Asheville and its surrounding communities became increasingly apparent. While the immediate devastation was visible, with downed trees and damaged homes, a more subtle but equally impactful set of challenges began to emerge in the months and years that followed.

Ongoing Challenges

One of the most pressing issues was mental health. The trauma of experiencing such a powerful storm lingered long after the winds had died down. Many residents found themselves grappling with anxiety and depression, struggling to come to terms with their experiences. Local mental health professionals reported an increase in demand for counseling services, with many people seeking support to cope with their feelings of loss and uncertainty. "It's not just about the physical damage," explained Dr. Lisa Mitchell, a psychologist in Asheville. "The emotional scars can be just as deep, if not deeper. People are still processing what happened."

Support groups began to form, offering safe spaces for residents to share their stories and feelings. These gatherings became lifelines for many, allowing them to express their fears and frustrations in an environment of understanding. "Being able to talk about our experiences helped me feel less isolated," shared one participant, a mother of two whose home had been significantly damaged. "I realized I wasn't alone in this."

Infrastructure repair also emerged as a significant concern. The hurricane had exposed weaknesses in the region's preparedness, leading to increased scrutiny of local infrastructure. Roads, bridges, and utilities had suffered considerable damage, prompting discussions about long-term improvements. "We were lucky that the storm didn't cause more widespread devastation," said Mark Stevens, the city's director of public works. "But we can't ignore the fact that some of our systems need serious upgrades."

Residents became more vocal about their needs, advocating for better drainage systems and stronger building codes. Town hall meetings filled with concerned citizens led to initiatives focused on enhancing the community's resilience against future storms. "We need to invest in infrastructure that can withstand whatever nature throws our. way," asserted one community leader. "It's not just about recovery; it's about preparing for the future."

Insurance claims presented another hurdle for many families. Navigating the complexities of insurance policies became a source of frustration and stress. Residents often found themselves at odds with insurance companies, facing delays and denials as they sought to recover financial losses. "The insurance process was a nightmare," said Amanda Thompson, reflecting on her family's experience. "We had to fight to get what we were owed, and it took months to get everything sorted out." This struggle added another layer of stress for families already coping with the emotional and physical toll of the storm.

Changes in the Community

In the years following Hurricane Helene, Asheville began to adapt in significant ways. The community came together to address the challenges they faced, leading to meaningful changes in local policies and practices. An emphasis on preparedness became a cornerstone of community planning. Schools introduced educational programs focused on emergency readiness, teaching students about the importance of having emergency kits and knowing evacuation routes. "We want our kids to feel empowered and informed," explained Principal Sarah Allen of Asheville Middle School. "Knowledge is a crucial part of safety."

Community organizations stepped up to provide resources and support for residents, creating a network of aid that extended beyond immediate recovery efforts. Nonprofits focused on disaster preparedness and mental health became more prevalent, addressing the ongoing needs of residents. "We learned that recovery isn't a sprint; it's a marathon," said Maria Gonzalez, director of a local nonprofit. "We need to be there for our community in the long haul."

Asheville also began to invest in green infrastructure, recognizing the role that nature plays in mitigating the impacts of storms. Initiatives such as creating more green spaces, planting trees, and improving drainage systems became priorities for city planners. "Nature can be our ally in times of crisis," said environmental activist James Brooks. "By restoring natural landscapes, we can reduce flooding and improve overall community resilience."

Reflections on Nature

The relationship between Asheville residents and their environment underwent a transformation in the wake of Hurricane Helene. The storm served as a stark reminder of the power of nature, prompting many to reconsider their connection to the land and the mountains that surrounded them. Community discussions about climate change and environmental stewardship became more prominent, with residents advocating for sustainable practices and policies.

"Helene opened our eyes to the reality of climate change and its impacts," said local environmentalist Emma Parker. "We can no longer afford to ignore the signs. We need to be proactive in protecting our environment." As a result, community groups began organizing clean-up efforts in local parks and waterways, emphasizing the importance of preserving the natural beauty that had always drawn residents to Asheville.

Moreover, the experience of the hurricane brought people closer to the land they inhabited. Many residents began to appreciate the delicate balance between humanity and nature, understanding that their actions had consequences for the environment. Gardening, local farming, and sustainability initiatives gained traction as more people sought to reconnect with the land. "We started a community garden to help provide fresh produce and promote local food systems," said Ana Martinez. "It's a small step, but it brings us together and reminds us of the beauty of what we have."

In the years following Hurricane Helene, Asheville emerged from the storm with a renewed sense of purpose and connection. The ongoing challenges served as catalysts for growth, prompting residents to advocate for a more resilient future. The bond forged through shared experiences became a testament to the community's strength as they faced the long-term effects of the hurricane together.

While the scars of the storm remained, the stories of recovery, adaptation, and reflection showcased the indomitable spirit of Asheville and its residents.

In navigating the complexities of post-hurricane life, they found not only resilience but also a profound appreciation for the environment and their place within it.

Chapter 7: Current Living Conditions in Asheville

Community Today

Asheville has transformed remarkably in the years following Hurricane Helene, emerging as a community that has learned, adapted, and thrived. The physical scars left by the hurricane have faded, replaced by new homes and businesses that reflect a commitment to resilience and sustainability. The streets, once battered by flooding and wind, now hum with activity as residents enjoy a vibrant cultural scene celebrating local art, music, and cuisine.

The commitment to rebuilding has been evident in both the public and private sectors. Local government initiatives have led to substantial infrastructure improvements, ensuring the city is better equipped to handle future storms. Many neighborhoods have seen upgrades to drainage systems designed to mitigate flooding, which was a significant issue during Helene. Enhanced roadways, improved traffic flow, and resilient public transport systems have made navigating the city safer and more efficient, enabling residents to go about their daily lives with greater peace of mind.

Community events and initiatives have flourished, driven by a collective desire to celebrate resilience and unity. Local farmers' markets are brimming with fresh produce, and community gardens thrive in many neighborhoods, promoting sustainable practices and food security. Events like the annual "Asheville Strong" festival bring residents together to commemorate their journey, offering a platform for local artists and businesses to showcase their talents. This commitment to community spirit has invigorated Asheville, creating a rich tapestry of interconnectedness that is both uplifting and empowering.

Future Preparedness

The prevailing attitude towards future storms in Asheville is one of preparedness and vigilance. Residents have developed a heightened awareness of the importance of emergency planning, fostering a culture where preparedness is viewed not just as a necessity, but as a shared responsibility. Neighborhood associations have implemented regular training sessions on emergency response, encouraging residents to engage in drills that prepare them for various scenarios.

Schools have integrated disaster preparedness into their curricula, teaching children how to stay safe and respond appropriately during emergencies. Parents, too, are taking active roles in preparing their families for potential disasters, ensuring every household has a plan in place. "I want my kids to feel safe and empowered," said local mom Jenna

Collins, who has led workshops on creating family emergency plans. "Knowledge is power, and we want to be ready for anything."

The local government has invested in community-wide initiatives aimed at improving response times and resource distribution during emergencies. This includes the establishment of local emergency response teams comprised of trained volunteers, who are ready to assist neighbors in need. Asheville's embrace of technology has also played a pivotal role; many residents now utilize smartphone apps to receive real-time alerts and updates about weather conditions and emergency resources.

Personal Reflections

Reflecting on their experiences, many Asheville residents cherish the bonds formed in the wake of Hurricane Helene. Stories of shared hardship and resilience have woven a narrative of hope and strength that resonates throughout the community. Neighbors who once exchanged pleasantries now share deep friendships forged in adversity. The relationships built during the recovery process have led to a network of support that extends beyond the immediate aftermath of the hurricane.

"Living through that storm changed my perspective," said longtime resident Thomas Jenkins. "It made me realize how important it is to be connected to those around you. We've built something beautiful out of a terrible situation." This sentiment is echoed throughout the community, as many residents take pride in the lessons learned and the relationships strengthened during the recovery.

The experience of rebuilding has also prompted a renewed appreciation for the natural environment surrounding Asheville. Many residents have become more involved in environmental advocacy, working to protect the landscapes that make their home unique. Initiatives focused on reforestation and conservation have gained traction, with community members volunteering their time to restore local ecosystems affected by the storm. "We've seen firsthand what nature can do, and it's inspired us to take better care of our environment," noted Emma Parker, a local environmentalist.

As Asheville continues to move forward, the lessons learned from Hurricane Helene remain at the forefront of residents' minds. While the community has rebuilt and adapted, they remain aware of the ever-changing climate and its potential threats. This consciousness has fostered a spirit of collaboration, ensuring that as the city evolves, it does so with resilience, preparedness, and a profound sense of community at its heart.

The journey of recovery is ongoing, and the scars of the past have paved the way for a brighter future. Residents approach their lives with optimism, fortified by the knowledge that they are not only survivors but also a community capable of rising to any challenge that lies ahead. As they gather in parks, cafes, and homes, conversations flow freely, centered around plans for the future, new businesses, and upcoming community events. In this vibrant setting, Asheville stands as a testament to the strength of the human spirit and the power of unity in the face of adversity.

Conclusion

The legacy of Hurricane Helene endures in Asheville, shaping both the physical landscape and the community's fabric. The storm catalyzed change, prompting residents to reflect on their vulnerability and the strength found in unity. Lessons learned about preparedness, resilience, and community have left an indelible mark on individual lives and the collective consciousness.

As Asheville thrives, it stands as a beacon of hope for future generations. The collaboration and determination that emerged in the storm's aftermath exemplify humanity's capacity for resilience. Residents now approach life with respect for nature and a commitment to preparedness.

To readers, the story of Hurricane Helene encourages embracing resilience and fostering community bonds. The shared experiences of Asheville's people underscore the importance of preparation for challenges, no matter how daunting. Future generations can draw inspiration from this narrative, understanding that strength lies in unity and peace of mind in preparedness. By nurturing connections, sharing knowledge, and supporting one another, communities can face tomorrow's uncertainties with courage and hope.

Made in the USA
Columbia, SC
06 December 2024

48439977R00028